Property Pro[illegible]d

A play

Lynn Brittney

ISBN 0 573 12201 6

Please see page iv for further copyright information

CHARACTERS

Simkins
Carol Benson-Brown
Smith
Traffic Warden

The action of the play takes place in an office

Time: the present

Other plays by Lynn Brittney
published by Samuel French Ltd:

A Different Way To Die
Have A Nice Day
The Last Wife

PROPERLY PROCESSED

The set is a fairly spartan office. There are some filing cabinets, and a desk and a chair. Two plastic chairs and a low coffee table are positioned DR. *On the coffee table are some old magazines and an upright container, facing the audience. In the container are number cards. The number fifty-three is displayed*

As the play opens, Simkins, a nondescript man in a suit, is filing

Ms Carol Benson-Brown enters R, *looking slightly bewildered. She is dressed in a power suit and carries a briefcase*

Carol Excuse me. I seem to have had a black-out, or something. Could you possibly send for a doctor?

Simkins (*looking round from his filing*) Do you have a number?

Carol (*confused*) Pardon?

Simkins (*indicating the coffee table*) You have to take a number, otherwise I can't deal with your request.

Carol You don't seem to understand. I'm not one of your clients. I'm asking for emergency assistance.

Simkins But you are.

Carol What?

Simkins You are one of my clients. Everyone who comes through that door is one of my clients.

Carol (*getting irritable*) Look, I don't even know what this place is. In fact, I don't even know how I got here. That is the problem. I'm ill. Can't you understand.

Simkins I must say that you don't look ill. In fact, I would state categorically that you are not ill. We don't get ill people coming in here.

Carol What sort of rubbish are you talking! Just get on the telephone and call your company nurse or someone.

Simkins Ah, well. That is the problem. I couldn't, even if I felt the necessity, which I don't.

Carol Couldn't what?

Simkins Telephone.

Carol Are you being deliberately obstructive?

Simkins No, not at all. I just don't have a telephone.

Carol (*looking at the desk*) Good God.

Simkins Now, if you'll just take a number, we can get everything sorted out.

Carol I don't want a bloody number! What sort of an office is this, that doesn't have a telephone!

Simkins The sort of office that doesn't need a telephone. The sort of office that just deals with paperwork.

Carol Rubbish. There's no such thing.

Simkins I beg to differ, madam.

Carol Look, I've spent all my working life in an office, and there is no such thing as an office that can do without telecommunications.

Simkins You seem to be feeling better, if I may say.

Carol (*sitting down; thrown slightly*) Well, I'm not. I still don't know how I got here. There is a—(*she struggles to remember*) great gap in my memory. Can't you understand? I've got amnesia or something. I need assistance.

Simkins I'm afraid you're beyond assistance, Miss Benson-Brown.

Carol How did you know my name?

Simkins In the same way that I know you're beyond assistance. You see, this may come as a shock to you, but no-one can help you now, because you are dead.

Carol (*hyperventilating a little, then pulling herself together and rising purposefully*) Look, I don't know what your problem is, but I've obviously come to the wrong place for help. I'll just leave now. Sorry to have troubled you.

She exits R *and then re-enters almost immediately in a state of controlled panic*

Why is that door locked? (*She lets out a high pitched shriek and assumes a karate combat position*)

Simkins jumps backwards and looks shocked

I have to warn you that I am highly trained in unarmed combat. There is no point in trying to assault me. I'm much fitter and probably stronger than you are.

Simkins Assault you! Bless my soul, Miss, I wouldn't dream of doing such a thing! Whatever made you think that I would?

Carol Look. The door is locked.

Simkins Of course. It's only an entrance door. You can't exit by it. To exit you have to go that way. (*He points* L)

Carol Oh, why didn't you say that in the first place, you stupid man!

She rushes off L *and re-enters, almost immediately*

(*In rising panic*) That door is locked too. Is this some sort of sick game?

Simkins Oh, dear me, you're in such a rush, aren't you? Of course that door is locked. You can only exit when you have been properly processed.

Carol (*on the verge of tears*) I told you before, I am not one of your clients!

Simkins And I told you before that you are. Look, come and sit down, (*he advances towards her*) and I'll explain.

Carol Don't touch me! Stay where you are!

Simkins I won't touch you, dear lady. Please take a seat and a number and we can begin.

Carol sits down warily, and Simkins comes over, takes the number fifty-three out of the holder and gives it to her. The number fifty-four is now on display

As I explained, (*he goes to the filing cabinet and takes out a file*) you are here, Miss Benson-Brown, because you are dead. (*He looks in the file*) Killed in a car crash while overtaking a lorry on a bend. Tut, tut. Always being in a rush really was the death of you, wasn't it? (*He smiles at his little joke*)

Carol (*dazed*) I—do remember pulling out to pass the lorry—but then I was here. And I thought I'd had a black-out. I don't remember anything else.

Simkins (*sympathetically*) No? Well, that's often the case with sudden deaths. Anyway, you've spent your statutory time in limbo, and now you've come through to us to be processed.

Carol Processed?

Simkins Yes. We have to sort out your details here and then pass you on to some sort of afterlife.

Carol Afterlife? You mean heaven and hell, that sort of thing?

Simkins Oh, I couldn't tell you about that, Miss Benson-Brown. I only do the processing.

Carol (*recovering her composure a little*) It's Ms.

Simkins Pardon?

Carol Ms, not Miss.

Simkins Of course. I should have realized that, being a bureaucrat yourself, you would be a stickler for detail. We've been looking forward to your arrival, Ms Benson-Brown—as a fellow administrative officer, so to speak.

Carol I am not an administrative officer. I am a Chief Planning Officer. I do not administer. I direct.

Simkins Well now, if we're drawing fine distinctions, I think you should say that you *were* a Chief Planning Officer, not that you are.

Carol (*deflated*) Yes.

Simkins (*gathering up a handful of forms and approaching*) Now. Here we are. This is a form *a*-seventy-six-*f*: affidavit of personal qualities. Here is your *h*-nine-six-two-*y* application for transfer to a higher plane; your *m*-two-three-nine-*z*—that's a statement of achievements and, of course, your *x*-ninety-nine—fond memories and loved ones. Would you like a pen?

Carol No, thank you, I always use my own. Are all these forms really necessary?

Simkins (*smiling*) I wonder how many times you've heard that question in your lifetime, Ms Benson-Brown? And what was your reply?

Carol (*awkwardly*) Er—yes—they are necessary in order to properly process the application.

Simkins Quite. (*He returns to his desk*) Now, I'll just leave you to it, there's no rush. (*He chuckles*) You have an eternity in which to fill in forms!

Carol opens her briefcase, takes out an expensive fountain pen and begins to read the forms

Carol Excuse me.

Simkins Yes?

Carol What does "Outline your personal qualities, both as you perceive them and as you think others perceive them" mean?

Simkins Well, I should have thought that it was self-explanatory. It means, write down what you think you are like as a person and what you think others think you're like.

Carol How on earth am I supposed to know what others think I'm like?

Simkins Come now. (*He picks up a file and reads*) Did you not say to your staff, the day before you died, "I know that you think I'm a hard woman, but it is of little consequence to me"? In fact, that particular sentence occurs several times over the years in our reports.

Carol What have you got in that file? (*She goes over to Simkins*) How dare you catalogue private conversations.

Simkins My dear Ms Benson-Brown, there are no such things as private conversations. Everything is known to us.

Carol This is intolerable. I want to see your superior.

Simkins I don't think that you do.

Carol (*scathing*) Aha! Now I' ve got you worried, haven't I. The typical response of a gutless underling. Oh, I've seen it so many times with my own staff. A bit of resistance from the general public and they crumble. It's always left to management to confront the problem clients. Fetch your superior now, I insist.

Simkins (*sighing*) Very well, if you insist. But I can assure you that you will find Mr Smith far less responsive than I. He's quite tough with uncooperative people.

Carol From what I've seen of this organisation thus far, I don't think that the word tough is in your vocabulary.

Simkins shakes his head and tuts, then exits L

Carol looks around furtively and then attempts to open the file that is lying on the desk. It becomes apparent that no amount of effort from her can prise open the covers. She picks up a paper knife and tries, but it still doesn't work. This begins to unnerve her and we hear a few little cries of frustration. She hears a sound, drops everything in its place on the desk and moves away R

Mr Smith enters, followed by Mr Simkin. Mr Smith is a sinister looking man who rarely smiles. His manner is condescending, his tone sarcastic

Mr Simkins seems rather cowed in his presence

Smith I understand there is some problem?

Carol (*slightly unnerved by his manner and appearance, but making a brave show of it*) Yes. Yes, there is.

Smith Well? Please outline your complaint and be brief. I do not have all day.

Carol (*aggrieved*) Just a minute! There's no need to use that patronising tone towards me. I shall take up as much time as I need in order to get a satisfactory answer to my questions.

Smith (*turning to Simkins with a grim smile*) I see that you were, for once, right to call me in, Simkins. There would appear to be an unnacceptable level of resistance here.

Simkins Yes, sir.

Smith (*advancing on Carol menacingly and delivering his speech with machine-gun rapidity*) So what is it, madam? Finding the forms too difficult to comprehend? Can't get your puny brain around the relatively simple concepts laid out in the documents? Feel that they are unnecessary and time-wasting? Feel that you are naturally destined for a beautiful afterlife without having to undergo the necessary formalities? *Well?*

Carol (*momentarily taken aback*) I—I—don't believe I am dead!

There is a silence whilst Mr Smith digests this piece of information and fixes her with a penetrating stare

Smith Oh, you don't believe you are dead?

Carol No.

Smith Well, that's easily remedied. Simkins! (*He snaps his fingers, without taking his eyes off Carol*)

Simkins quickly places the paper knife in his hand and Smith, equally quickly, grabs Carol, bends her over the desk and repeatedly stabs her. Carol screams as if she were being killed. Smith stops, stands up straight, fastidiously hands the knife back to Simkins and straightens his tie. Carol slumps to the floor

Carol You—you monster! You animal! (*She clutches her chest and then realizes there is no blood. She looks down the front of her shirt in amazement*)

Smith (*disinterested*) See? Quite dead. Dead as the proverbial dodo. Now, I take it that I may return to my more important work?

Carol (*breathing heavily*) Yes. (*She has a thought*) No. I have something else to ask you.

Smith Really, Miss Benson-Brown——

Simkins Ms, sir.

Smith What?

Simkins She prefers to be called Ms, sir.

Smith (*unimpressed*) Oh, really. Well, *Ms* Benson-Brown, what is this other matter which demands my attention?

Carol I want to know everything about the processing. (*She gathers herself up off the floor and straightens herself up. There is now an air of purpose about her*) As a fellow bureaucrat, I want to know all about your system. What you do—how you function. I'm interested.

Smith (*slightly flattered*) Really? Well, I think we can possibly accomodate you there. We're rather proud of our processing techniques here. We have the lowest turnover of all the processing departments.

Carol There are other departments, then?

Smith Oh, goodness, yes. (*He gestures towards the seats around the coffee table*) Would you like to take a seat and I'll explain our procedures.

Carol Thank you.

Smith (*warming to his subject*) Now, as I said, here we have the lowest turnover of all the departments. That means we process far fewer people than the others. Isn't that right, Simkins?

Simkins Yes, sir. The average is one hundred and twenty-two a week. We average fifty-six.

Smith Fifty-six.

Carol Is that good? Forgive me, but surely you should be processing people quickly, not slowly?

Smith Oh no! My dear lady, the whole point of this procedure is to cause the maximum amount of discomfort to the individual being processed.

Carol Why?

Smith To test you, of course! The client's degree of patience and amiability determines his or her level of afterlife.

Carol I see. So my attitude thus far has gone against me, is that what you're saying.

Smith We-ell. It doesn't look too good. But your chances are improving, that's all I can say. The ultimate decision doesn't rest with me, of course.

Carol Then with whom does it rest?

Smith What impeccable English. Dear lady, I thought you said you were a fellow bureaucrat? With whom would you imagine the final decision rests?

Carol (*realising*) A committee?

Smith Of course!

Carol And is it possible to put one's case, personally, to this committee?

Smith and Simkins draw in their breath and shake their heads

Smith Did you allow such a thing at planning committee meetings? No, of course you didn't. The written facts are placed in front of the committee for them to consider.

Carol I see. And how are these facts assembled?

Smith Simkins! I think this is where you take over.

Simkins Yes, sir. (*He comes forward and brings the file*) We have various documents that are presented. There's the grief quotient, of course.

Carol The what?

Smith Grief quotient. We measure on a scale of one to one hundred the level of grief felt at your death.

Carol And what did I rate?

Simkins Three.

Carol Three!

Simkins Yes. Even Adolf Hitler managed eight.

Smith Dear, dear. Not a good start.

Carol But that's impossible! What about my mother?

Simkins (*looking in the file*) Never liked you very much, apparently. Said you were a difficult baby and you never improved.

Carol What about Nigel? The man I lived with?

Simkins Married his secretary three weeks after you died.

Carol Bastard.

Simkins The manageress of your favourite clothes shop exhibited some grief. Apparently you spent quite a lot of money in her shop. She even sent some flowers to the funeral. Apart from that, there's very little really.

Smith Then, of course, there are the affidavits as to your character that you amass throughout your life.

Carol (*bitterly*) I suppose they're all dreadful too. (*Aside*) I can't believe he married his secretary.

Simkins (*reading*) Well… (*He produces a large wodge of paper*) Mostly, there are statements from people whose planning applications were denied, on your recommendation.

Carol But that's hardly fair! It was my job to assess all planning applications on their merit. You're bound to get some disgruntled people, when they don't get their own way!

Smith Ah, but correct me if I'm wrong, but *you* weren't exactly fair, were you? Is it not true, Simkins, that certain property developers got their applications passed after you had accepted their bribes?

Carol I didn't take bribes!

Smith Simkins.

Simkins Yes, sir. We have on record here the following items. A planning consultancy for a Maclaren Development Corporation worth £20,000 a year; seven foreign holidays in timeshare villas owned by various property developers; a new car, courtesy of another developer. Shall I go on?

Smith Quite an impressive list.

Carol (*sighing*) You obviously don't understand the way that local government works. I really didn't have any choice.

Smith (*sarcastically*)Really?

Carol Look. I am—was—one of only eight female Chief Planning Officers in the country. Being female was enough of a handicap to promotion in a male-dominated world. Being honest would have been totally unacceptable.

Smith I'm sorry?

Carol *All* the other Chief Officers, without exception, took hand-outs, bribes, sweeteners, whatever you want to call them. In order for me to be elevated to their ranks I had to be—well—the same. Otherwise, I would never have been promoted. I mean, you can't expect them to allow someone into an exclusive club who doesn't abide by the rules, can you?

Smith But surely you achieved promotion on your merits, Ms Benson-Brown?

Carol Oh, don't be silly. No-one ever gets promoted in local government on merit. One gets promotion because one—bends—because one achieves the results that councillors want, without compromising the position of the officers.

Simkins (*writing*) Could you go over that last part again? I'm afraid I haven't got it all.

Carol Are you writing this down?

Smith Of course he is. It all forms part of your submission to the committee, you know.

Carol Oh, for goodness sake! I wish you had given me some prior notice. I would have phrased things better.

Smith You're doing admirably, Ms Benson-Brown. Do carry on. Simkins and I are finding this exposé of local government quite illuminating. I'm sure the more that the committee understands, the better it will be for your case. Could you explain the bit about achieving results for the councillors without compromising the officers? I'm afraid that I am not clear on that point.

Carol (*irritated by his stupidity*) Look. The whole point of local government is that the councillors, the elected members, the *amateurs*, spend their time trying to get the officers, the professional administrators, to do things that are recommended by political party policy and are neither reasonable, nor, for the most part, practical. So, therefore, a good Chief Officer has to find a way of thwarting the councillor's desires without seeming to be deliberately obstructive. It's called passive resistance. (*Proudly*) In my time, I have been responsible for delaying action on a particular decision for so long that the entire council has changed due to a general election and the action was no longer necessary. I certainly went up in my colleagues' estimation for that, I can tell you.

Smith Magnificent!

Simkins Very commendable.

Smith Of course, you are the first local government officer that we have processed through this department. We'd had a bit of a reshuffle, you see. Previously, we dealt with vandals and petty criminals. So, from what you say, we can look forward to an eternity of dealing with bureaucratic corruption, eh?

Carol Oh, dear. You really do take a simplistic view of things, don' t you? Not *everyone* in local government is corrupt.

Simkins (*disappointed*) No? Oh, that is a shame.

Carol Well, there isn't the opportunity, for a start. I mean, you have to be in a position of power before the public can exert influence over your decision.

Smith Oh, quite.

Carol And sometimes, if you go very high up, it is necessary to be completely honest.

Smith Oh, come now. That goes against everything you have just told us.

Carol No. No. There are many instances of Chief Executives—or Town Clerks as they are sometimes called—being incorruptible.

Smith May one ask why? I should have thought that a Chief Executive was in the supreme position to take every advantage.

Carol Oh no. Too visible. A Chief Executive has too many dealings with the media, really, to risk his position with shady deals. Anyway, some people in local government feel that it is a positive requirement that Chief Executives are as stupid as possible. Certainly, most councillors are happier with a dim Chief Executive. Easier to manipulate, you see. And there's another point: most Chief Executives have nothing to bargain with. It's the Chief Officers who can offer lucrative contracts or development permissions and the like that are the targets for big business. Housing, Planning, Recreation, even Social Services.

Simkins Libraries?

Carol (*scornfully*) No! Who is going to bribe a Chief Librarian? Some author who wants three more copies of his books on the shelves? Hardly.

Smith Well. This is all valuable background material for our future work. Thank you, Ms Benson-Brown.

Carol I believe that *everyone* is open to persuasion of some sort.

Smith (*getting up and obviously wanting to draw the conversation to a close*) Really? Well, thank you, Ms Benson-Brown, you've been most helpful. I'm afraid I must get on with my work now. If you'll just fill in those forms that Simkins gave you, we can process you without further ado.

Carol Including you.

Smith Pardon?

Carol I'm sure that I could offer you something that would— remove the necessity for all this form filling—and obtain a favourable response from the committee as to my eventual destination?

Smith (*permitting himself a wry smile*) My dear lady, are you offering me a bribe?

Carol If that's how you care to look at it.

Smith Did you hear that, Simkins?

Simkins Yes, sir. Most amusing, sir.

Smith Yes. Most amusing. What, Ms Benson-Brown, do you possibly imagine you can offer us that we would have any use for? You and I, and Simkins here, are all dead. We have no use for money, cars, holidays, fancy clothes, or any of the other ridiculous things that you have accepted in your time on earth. You, my dear lady, have no means anyway, of procuring those things for us. Those are material possessions from the real world which you no longer inhabit. And God forbid, should you be considering an offer of sexual favours, let me assure you that neither Simkins nor I have felt the urge to touch a woman for over six thousand years!

Simkins Even longer in my case, sir. I never fancied it much when I was alive, either.

Smith Thank you, Simkins. I think we have made our point.

Carol I think that you should credit me with a little more sense than that Mr—er, what is your name?

Smith Smith, my name is Smith, madam.

Carol You're quite wrong, you know. I *do* have something that you are interested in.

Smith Enlighten me.

Carol My bureaucratic skills. Finely honed over twenty years in local government. You're quite proud of your department and its work, aren't you?

Smith Justifiably so. As I told you, we have the lowest turnover of any of the departments.

Carol Ah, but that is when you were processing—what was it? Petty criminals and vandals. Now you're dealing with local government officials. The next person who comes through that door could go through these forms like a dose of salts and be out of that door in a flash. Then what happens to your precious average turnover? Local government officers are used to form-filling, they respect bureaucracy, they're not petty criminals who are intimidated by bureaucratic procedures. I bet that half your previous clients were semi-literate. Am I right?

Smith Er—yes.

Carol Well, you *need me*. I can do a management review of this place and devise a system which will paralyse the whole process. Simkins! Check my file. What does it say about my time in the Midlands as Senior Conservation Officer?

Simkins (*leafing through the file; reading*) It says that during your time there you created three separate systems for processing conservation area planning applications, which caused the average time of applications to be extended by at least eleven months. You also made forty-two staff redundant and re-wrote eighty-seven job descriptions so that a further twenty-six staff resigned. It took an outside consultancy to put the department back together after you left.

Smith (*grabbing the file*) Let me see that!

Carol I rest my case.

Smith (*muttering*) Eighty-seven job descriptions—twenty-six staff left. (*Flabbergasted*) Madam, I had no idea you were so talented!

Carol Exceptional work, eh?

Smith Exceptional.

Carol Now, do you admit that I have something that you want?

Smith I—I don't know. This is an irregular procedure. Quite outside my sphere of experience.

Carol Let me convince you. (*She opens up her briefcase and takes out a clipboard and starts making notes*) For a start. Why are you doing everything manually? If you want to intimidate people, why aren't you computerised? Nothing puts the fear of God in people as much as a computer. And you certainly can't deal with local government personnel without one. Computers are part of their religion. They believe in them implicitly, even when they go wrong. Secondly, why are you providing magazines? Any form of diversion is out. I don't—didn't—allow them in any of my department's waiting rooms, nor any pictures on the walls. There's nothing like staring at a blank wall to reduce a person's resistance to authority.

Simkins But they're totally uninteresting magazines. Look! Transport Weekly. Pig Breeder's Gazette. The Journal of the Psoriasis Society.

Carol It doesn't matter! Some little twerp will find something interesting in one of them. Get rid of them. These seats are too comfortable. What you want are hard wooden benches. No backs or arms and not long enough for anyone to lie down on. I learnt that trick when I did a spell of work experience as a youngster in a Social Security office.

Smith Admirable.

Carol Now. As to staff interaction with clients.

Simkins Pardon?

Carol The way that you deal with the people who come in here.

Simkins Oh.

Carol You deal with them too quickly. The idea of the numbering system is a good one. But the true value of that lies in the fact that you create the impression that taking a number entitles the client to a place in a *queue*. You should display a sign over there which explains that you are presently dealing with a lower number. It would be at least ten numbers before the one here. (*She indicates the coffee table*) I suppose they come in one at a time, do they?

Smith Well, yes. We couldn't properly process several people at once.

Carol No. Quite. Anyway, a sense of isolation is extremely valuable in dealing with the public. Let two or more of them gather together and they start feeding off each other's grievances and before you know where you are, they are banding together to resist the system.

Smith You really are very skilled at this.

Carol I know. I have spent my whole career refining the techniques for creating human misery. I know whereof I speak. Now. These forms are really too easy.

Simkins They are?

Carol Oh, much too easy. You ask only a very few questions and give people far too much space to write quite a lot of irrelevant rubbish. In my opinion, one should design a form which goes for the maximum amount of frustration by putting in lots of questions that are difficult to understand. Lots of cross-references.

Smith How do you mean?

Carol (*drawing it out and showing him*) Well, look. You ask question A and then say, if the answer is "No", then proceed to question C, if the answer is "Yes", then proceed to question G. That way you can guarantee that the form filler will get lost in the wrong line of questioning and have to start all over again with a fresh form. Of course, it means extra expenditure on paper.

Smith Marvellous. Dear lady, it's so simple. Don't worry about our budget.

Carol Then, for all the questions you allow very little space for answers so that they have to write in margins, etc., and the whole end result is such a mess that it leaves them feeling utterly humiliated. There is also a school of thought that prefers multiple choice questions, where one just ticks the relevant answer. But those really have to be put together by an expert, because one really needs to provide a multiple choice of totally unsatisfactory answers so that the person filling in the form is unable to make a choice. I'm afraid I would not feel confident in designing such a form. But if ever a man called Geoff Thomas dies and appears here in the near future, I can highly recommend his skills. He produced a form for me for grant applicants and we reduced the number of grants awarded for loft insulation by over fifty per cent because most of the elderly people applying for them couldn't understand the forms! (*She laughs*)

Smith (*thinking hard and signalling Simkins over*) I have been most impressed with what I have just heard, Ms Benson-Brown. I wonder if Mr Simkins and I might have a private conference for a moment, if you would excuse us?

Carol Of course. (*She goes and sits down by the coffee table and looks smug*)

Smith and Simkins turn their backs on the audience and confer silently for about thirty seconds. Smith then comes over to her

Smith May I call you Carol?

Carol Please do, Mr Smith.

Smith Carol. I hope you will forgive me for not realising your outstanding potential when you arrived earlier. I think I speak for Mr Simkins and myself when I state that we are both now your most fervent admirers.

Simkins (*nodding agreement; murmuring*) Hear, hear.

Smith What I would like to suggest now, is a little revolutionary for us, but something that I hope you may find acceptable. Carol, how would you like to stay here? Work here alongside Simkins and help us process your fellow local government officers?

Carol Well—it's not what I had in mind—I must be frank, Mr Smith. When I suggested a management reveiw I had rather hoped it would speed my passage into the afterlife.

Smith Ms Benson-Brown—Carol. I am now going to break one of our cardinal rules here and divulge some information about the afterlife.

Simkins Oh, sir, do you think that you should?

Smith Exceptional circumstances dictate exceptional measures, Simkins. I take full responsibility.

Simkins Yes, sir.

Smith Carol—the afterlife is—well—it's boring. In your case, I'm afraid, it would be a great grey nothing, like a giant wet fog, in which you would wander forever, with only your own thoughts for company.

Carol Oh, God.

Smith Yes, I'm afraid so.

Carol But I thought that perhaps we could do a deal?

Smith That would be the best deal that we could do for you, alas. The alternative would be too horrible for me to describe to you. The place that you were originally destined for, and undoubtedly would have been sent to by the committee, was a level of afterlife reserved for those who have dedicated their lives to make other people's lives a misery.

Carol (*understanding*) Which I did.

Smith Which you did. The grey nothing that I described is for truly boring people that never contributed anything to life. It's the best we could offer you in the circumstances. Other than, of course, my suggestion that you work here.

He takes her by the arm and paces across the stage with her

Just think Carol. Here, in this office, you would be able to do what you enjoy doing the most—frustrating the public. Here you would have power—be able to assert yourself whenever you liked. You could create a wonderfully difficult processing system and you could change it as often as you liked. Carol, I'm offering you promotion over Mr Simkins.

Simkins (*shocked*) Oh, sir!

Smith Quiet, Simkins. Face it, man. You've been in this job too long. We need some fresh blood. Some new ideas. We need to toughen up. Carol, we need you!

Carol (*seized with a kind of fervour*) Yes! I'll take it!

Smith Good girl! (*He pumps her hand up and down*) Simkins, congratulate your new boss.

Simkins (*sulkily going over and shaking her hand*) Congratulations.

Smith Welcome to the team, Carol. I expect great things of you. The committee expects great things of you!

Suddenly, a slightly dazed Traffic Warden comes through the entrance door. He pauses and clutches on the back of a chair, and then speaks

Traffic Warden Excuse me, I feel rather faint. Could I have a glass of water?

Smith Carol—your public awaits. Go get 'em!

Carol flexes her fingers, takes in a deep breath and marches forward

Carol Have you got a number? (*She looks back at Smith and Simkins who both give her the thumbs-up sign*)

Traffic Warden Pardon?

Carol Are you deaf? I said, "Have you got a number?" (*She shouts*) And stand up straight when I'm talking to you.

Black-out

FURNITURE AND PROPERTY LIST

Further dressing may be added at the director's discretion

On stage: Filing cabinets. *In them:* files

Desk. *On it:* forms, files, pen, large wodge of paper, paper knife

Chair

Coffee table. *On it:* old magazines, upright container with number cards

2 plastic chairs

Off stage: Briefcase. *In it:* expensive fountain pen, clipboard (**Carol**)

LIGHTING PLOT

Property fittings required: nil
Interior. The same throughout

To open: Overall general lighting

Cue 1 **Carol**: "…I'm talking to you." (Page 20)
Black-out

Printed by
The Kingfisher Press, London NW10